HOW COULD IT BE?

BY XIOMARA RODRIGUEZ

DORRANCE
PUBLISHING CO
EST. 1920
PITTSBURGH, PENNSYLVANIA 15238

Dorrance Publishing Co
585 Alpha Drive
Pittsburgh, PA 15238
Visit our website at *www.dorrancebookstore.com*

ISBN: 978-1-6393-7337-6
eISBN: 978-1-6393-7725-1

HOW COULD IT BE?

DEDICATION

I dedicate this book to my husband of forty years, David M. Wolfe, who has been my love, my soulmate, my support, and my rock. He truly believes in me, and without him, this book would not have been accomplished.

To my daughters, Kishly and Shannon; my grandkids, Felix and Mariah; and to my great-grandkids, Sadie, Keenan, and Onyx, you guys fill my life with joy. Thank you so much.

To all my family and friends, thank you so much for your support.

FOREWORD

MORE THAN FORTY YEARS AGO, I met a very beautiful, charismatic, engaging woman who I would soon come to realize is the love of my life. I soon understood that she has a way of weaving an interesting and entertaining story out of almost any situation. Her descriptions will make any story come alive in the imagination. You are about to start a journey into the imagination of Xiomara filled with unexpected twists and turns. You will probably have occasion to say, "What just happened?" I hope you enjoy every step of the journey, as I have for the last forty years. Enjoy.

CHAPTER 1
SISTERS, REALLY

I thought today was going to be an easy day. At least, when I woke up this morning that was what I thought. But it has not turned out that way.

Let me put things in perspective. About a year ago, I was promoted to lieutenant of the Homicide Department of the San Francisco Police Department. I was ecstatic; I thought that with this promotion I could take things a bit easier.

But no, things have just gone totally off the rails. As I sat in my office, first thing this morning I get a call from dispatch. An FBI agent has been shot in the SFPD parking garage. She is severely wounded, and the kicker to all this is, wait for it, she looks just like me! At least, that is what dispatch knows. The agent has been transported to the hospital.

Not soon after the call from dispatch comes the call from the chief of police and the mayor. The question is, how come an FBI agent was shot in our garage, and how is it possible that she looks just like me?

And all this is happening before my second cup of coffee.

I immediately go to my office to see where we stand. The officer that was present at the time of the shooting, Officer Vargas, has been on the force for more than ten years, and we have known each other for about five of those ten years. So, there cannot be a mistake in his recognition of who I am.

"Hi Vargas, tell me where we stand on the shooting," I said in a soft voice. (What I really wanted to say was "How the hell could you confuse me with someone else?" But I kept my composure and listened carefully.)

"Okay, tell me what happened," I said.

"Lieutenant, I was walking toward my patrol car when I saw a female that looked just like you. I swear she seemed to be your twin sister. She had long hair like you; she walked just like you. I mean, Lieutenant, I thought it was you, so I called out, and she seemed to turn toward me when out of nowhere this car approached her, and the next thing I heard were three shots, and down she went. I ran toward her and called it out. I really thought it was you, so I called it out that you had been shot. When the paramedics arrived and turned her over, I saw her FBI badge and her gun. So, I got a look at her credentials, and I took a picture of it."

"First thing, did you get a look at the shooter?"

"No, the car windows were limo tinted. I couldn't see anything inside. What I did see was a man's hand pointing a .9 mm. I want to say it was a Beretta. He had what looked like a military type of tattoo, on his wrist. He seemed to be Caucasian."

"Good. That's a good start. What type of car, and did you get the tags?" I asked.

"Yes, a black Mercedes, I want to say 2017. California tags. I was able to get the last four of the tag, J243."

"Good job. Run the plate and see what you get. Now, tell me about the agent."

"She is about your height, dark hair like you, thin build, wore a dark color pants suit. It looked like the ones you use. Caucasian, no visible tattoos, just a scar on her right wrist, as if she had been cut with barbwire."

"Are you sure she looked like me?" I asked.

"Oh, yes, Lieutenant, I could swear she was your twin. I took a picture of her and her credentials just before they put her in the ambulance and took her away."

"Can I see it?"

"Sure."

Vargas pulls out his phone and shows me the photo. The person in the picture really did look a lot like me. I wondered why the FBI had transformed an agent to look like me. Her name is Francesca Morris. This was very disturbing. Here is an FBI agent that looks like me, shot in the SFPD garage.

There are so many questions: Why does she look like me? What is behind that image? Was she shot because someone thought she was me? If so, who could that be? I know I have put away a lot of people, but who could want me dead?

But there is also the possibility that she was followed and shot because of an investigation the FBI was conducting. And lastly, why was she in our garage?

Too many questions and no answers.

After getting the name of the hospital she was been transferred to, I asked Officer Vargas to leave. Then I contacted the chief and provided the information I had just obtained from Vargas.

I contacted the hospital for an update on Agent Morris. I was advised that she was still in surgery. I asked them to notify me as soon as she was able to talk. This was a case that I wanted to handle myself.

Then I contacted the local FBI office. I was transferred to the assistant special agent in charge, who informed me that Agent Morris was the special agent in charge. He also stated that they were aware of the shooting and had sent an agent to the hospital.

He said he could not say anything else over the phone and recommended that we meet in person. I told him he could come over to my office, and we set the time for late in the afternoon. I also told him that I would send a couple of officers to the hospital for her protection.

After all that was set, I found myself with more questions than answers. The ringing of the phone brought me back to the moment.

"Lt. Sparks, yes, yes, thank you I will be heading that way shortly. In the meantime, I am sending two officers to be placed in front of her room. Yes, around the clock until we find out what is going on."

"Operations, this is Lieutenant Jane Sparks. I need two officers sent to the hospital immediately to guard room 255, the room of the FBI agent that was shot here earlier. Except for her doctor and her nurse, no one else can go into the room. Make sure they get the name of the doctor and the nurses on all shifts. Yes, the personnel must identify themselves. I will be there shortly."

After hanging up, I knew that it was time for me to go and meet this woman who could be my twin.

A twenty-minute drive to the hospital. Boy, how much I hate hospitals. Since the death of my father, I have not been in one, and I really did not want to be in one now. But here I am. This trip better be worth it.

As I approached the room, I could see one of my officers arguing with a woman; she was about five, five, slight build, blond, wearing about four-inch heels and looking impeccably dressed.

As I approached, I could hear the officer say, "Ma'am, you can't go in there."

The woman angrily replied, "I am her wife. By law I have the right to be in there. Now move."

"That's okay, officer, I'll take it from here."

The woman turned to face me. She had amazingly expressive blue eyes; she was an incredibly beautiful woman.

"Hi, I'm Lieutenant Jane Sparks, SFPD," I said as I stretched out my hand to greet her.

"I am Sasha Dean. I am Fran's wife, and I have the right under the law to be advised of her medical status and to be by her side," she firmly stated.

"I understand, and we are not trying to keep anything from you, but you have to realize that your wife was shot in our garage, and we need to investigate, especially considering that she is an FBI agent."

Then suddenly, she stopped and looked at me like she had seen a ghost.

"Oh my God, you look like Fran! You guys could be twins. What is going on?" she said. It seemed like she was about to faint, but she regained her composure.

I held her by the elbow and guided her to a couple of chairs close by.

"Like I said, I am Lieutenant Jane Sparks from the SFPD. I would really like to understand what is going. You said your wife and I look alike? How can that be possible?" I asked.

I knew there was a resemblance. I had Googled Agent Morris just before I left the office, and right after I saw the photo on Officer Vargas phone, but I was not about to acknowledge that.

"I would like to know the same thing. Could I see your wrist, please?" she asked.

"Why?"

"Fran's right wrist was injured by barbwire some time back when she was chasing a suspect. That is a very distinguishing mark," she said.

I remembered what Vargas had said when he was describing her earlier.

"Could you please tell me more about Agent Morris," I said.

"Fran began in law enforcement with the NYPD, then she became an FBI agent. About six month ago, she was transferred to the San Francisco FBI office as the special agent in charge."

"There is no coincidence that woman that looks like me. But why was she shot in the SFPD garage?" I said.

"I don't understand what is going on."

"Neither do I. But we will figure all this out. I promise."

"If you don't have any more questions, could I please be allowed in the room with my wife?" she said.

"Of course." We walked back to the door, where the two officers were standing guard. "She is allowed to go in at any time."

As she walked in, she turned around and I could see the pain in her eyes. "Thank you."

After checking with the doctor about Agent Morris's condition, I left. As I was walking back to my car, I called my friend Claire Underwood, the chief medical examiner.

After I explained what was going on, she told me that I needed to get a subpoena for a DNA test. She would administer the test as soon as I got the subpoena. She said to let her know when I got it.

Because of the importance of the case, I was granted the subpoena, and the following day Claire and I were back at the hospital ready to do the DNA test.

Mrs. Dean-Morris was not incredibly happy about what was going on, but she understood that she had no choice in the matter. As I looked into the face of this woman for the very first time, I realized she did surprisingly look very much like me. It was surprisingly haunting.

Claire and I looked at each other in disbelief. How could it be possible for two women, from different backgrounds, who grew up in two totally different states look so much alike?

Claire took the blood that she needed for the test. Later, in the lab, she would draw my blood, and then in a few days, we will know the results.

Two days later, the test results came back. To our great surprise, the results indicated that Agent Morris and I were sisters, twin sisters from the same mother and father. How could this be possible?

CHAPTER 2
THE DNA

The DNA test had come back, and it revealed that Fran and I were sister. To boot, it showed we were twin sisters, that we had the same mother and father. But how was that possible.

What had happened? We needed to get to the bottom of this.

The first thing I did was go through all the boxes in my attic that belonged to my father and mother. I was hoping there was something there that could help us, considering that both of my parents were dead.

I asked Sasha to check in all of Fran's papers for anything that could help us. And we all prayed that Fran would recover so maybe she could help us.

A week had gone by since the shooting, and there were no clues about the shooting. We had not moved the case forward at all.

Then came a call from Sasha. Fran was awake and we could talk to her. This was good news on one side, but I did not know how she would react to the news that we were twin sisters.

Claire and I entered the room. Lying there, looking fragile, was my, until now, unknown sister. This was so strange; it was like looking in a mirror. I wondered what she was thinking, how she would react.

"Hi, I am Jane Sparks; it is … great to meet you," I said.

Fran stared at me, then she looked toward Sasha. You could see the surprise in her face, all the questions that were coming up. Then she spoke.

"Who are you, and why do you look like me? What is this; what are you trying to do? Sasha, some help here, please," she said.

"Fran, I don't know how to say this, but she is your twin sister. It was proven by a DNA test."

"That is crazy and impossible. I never had a sister, and I would know. Mom would not have given a daughter up for adoption. What is all this about? Who sent you? What are you trying to do?"

"I know how you feel; I had the same reaction. I even wondered why you had such extensive face surgery to look like me. But we did a DNA test, and it came back as positive for us as sisters. To top it, we are twin sisters."

"This is crazy! That is not possible! How did it happen?"

"That is what we need to find out. We need to get to the bottom of this. In addition, we need to find out why you got shot, There are too many questions and extraordinarily few answers. But first, we need to find out how we ended up being sisters and not knowing anything about each other."

"First of all, my MOTHER would have never given you up for adoption! She would have done everything that she could to keep us together."

"That is the problem. I was not adopted, as far as I know. If I were, my mother would have told me. There is something really wrong right here, and we need to find out what it is," I said.

"But the bottom line is, how do you know that we are sisters?" she said in a not very cordial tone.

I stalled for a few seconds before I answered.

"As your wife mentioned before, we conducted a DNA test that proved we are sisters. The DNA also established that we are from the same mother and father."

She was angry and confused at the same time. I could see it in her eyes. I felt so bad for her; if I was confused, she must be even more confused. Someone shoots her, and when she wakes up in the hospital, she finds out that, out of the blue, she has a twin sister that she never knew about.

I look at her with intensity. It is just strange to have your eyes look back at you. And I wasn't looking in a mirror.

I motioned to the other chair in the room and asked if I could sit and talk. The answer did not come from Fran but from Sasha. So, I pulled the chair closer to the bed and sat. The silence in the room was overwhelming. Then Fran spoke:

"Okay, if the DNA test proved that we are sisters, then we have to find out how this happened?"

And once again there was silence.

"I guess we are going to have to work together to solve this mystery and find out who shot you and why. But right now, the most important thing is for you to get better; then we can tackle everything," I said in the softest voice I could muster.

"Well, we have a small problem," Sasha said, "Fran's mom arrives from New York City in a few hours, and she is going to be shocked when she sees you."

This did put a twist on everything, but it was a twist that should have been expected. It also brought some fear to my heart. If this woman was my real biological mother, I wondered why she gave me up. Why had she kept Fran and not me? So many questions were dancing in my brain, and I was sure the same was going on in Fran's head. Now we just needed to wait until Fran's mother arrived.

CHAPTER 3
THE TIME HAD COME

It was about 7:00 A.M. I was in my apartment from where I could see the bay. I was having a cup of coffee when my phone rang. It was Sasha. She had spoken to Sarah, and she was willing to meet with me in the hospital. She was just as intrigued as the rest of us. I told her I would be there in an hour.

This was going to be an incredibly challenging meeting. I rushed to finish getting dress, and then I left for the hospital.

The San Francisco weather was ever changing. Today the fog was covering almost everything, the sky was gray, and it was cold. I wondered if this was a premonition of what was waiting for me at the hospital.

I arrived at the hospital with a head full of questions and with some trepidation. I had no idea what would happen. This was virgin ground for me.

All my life I just knew one father, George Sparks, who died five years ago, and my mother, AnnMarie. She passed away when I was a teen, and I was raised by my cop dad. He was an amazing and caring man.

But if these people were not my real parents, who were they? And if they were my real parents, then why did they give Fran up for adoption? Too many questions and no answers until I could speak to Sarah.

When I entered the room, Sarah was sitting right next to her daughter, holding her hand. Sasha was on the other side of the bed. There was one extra chair, at the foot of the bed. I guessed it was for me.

With trepidation in my heart, I approached Sarah. She stood up and walked toward me. She looked into my eyes, slowly touched my face, then she looked at my wrist. Once again, she looked into my eyes and said:

"What is this all about? Why do you look so much like my daughter? What kind of game are you playing?"

"I am not playing any games. This is me; this is who I have been all my life. A week ago, your daughter entered the garage of the SFPD. There, she was shot and immediately transported to the hospital. During this process, we discovered the similarities between your daughter and me. We did a DNA test and discovered that we are sisters, from the same father and mother. The question now is…" I hesitated. I really did not want to come out as thoughtless, but I had to know. "Are you our mother, or did you adopt Fran?"

That was not the way I wanted to approach the issue, but I just could not wait any longer.

Sarah held her daughter's hand even tighter; there were tears in her eyes, and she spoke:

"I DID NOT ADOPT Fran. I gave birth to her on June 12, 1976. In a hospital in New York City at three o'clock in the afternoon, and it was a very delicate birth. I only had one child in that birth, because if you had been born, then I would have never given you up."

I collapsed in the chair next to me, then my deepest fear came to the surface. I did not want to even think about it. But the truth was hiding in the words Sarah had just said.

"I was born on June 12, 1976, in a NYC hospital at 2:55 P.M. Both my mother and my uncle worked in the same hospital. My mother was a nurse; my uncle was an obstetrician," I said in an incredibly soft voice.

The realization that my mother and uncle could have done something so cruel was overwhelming, but I felt that maybe I was jumping to a conclusion.

"Sarah, do you remember the name of your doctor?" I asked.

"Of course, Dr. Kevin O'Dell. He also delivered my son, Tommy."

"Was there a nurse with him that day?" I asked.

"Yes, there was. She was new, and she was such a sweet woman."

I pulled out my phone and search my photos. I came across the only photo I had of my mother and showed it to Sarah.

"Is this the nurse you saw the day you gave birth to Fran?"

With shaking hands, Sarah took the phone and looked at the photo. Tears started to stream down her face; her hands began to shake. And then, she collapsed.

The next few hours were extremely hard for all of us. Sarah had been taken to the emergency room. Sasha went with her, leaving me alone with Fran, who wanted to get up and go with her mother, or maybe I should say, our mother. I felt the anger in Fran's eyes. She blamed me for her mother's collapse. She would blame me if something went terribly wrong with Sarah. For God's sake, I would blame myself. We both looked at each other, then Fran spoke.

"This scenario was in the back of your mind, right? That your mother and uncle took you the moment you were born."

"Yes, there weren't all that many scenarios here. One, my mother had us both and gave you up for adoption; two, your mother gave me up for adoption; or three, I was stolen," I said with a knot in my throat.

The last thought was the hardest for me to articulate. My mother had taken me at birth from my biological mother with the help of my uncle. But how could that have happened? Still more questions than answers.

In an act of total compassion, Fran motioned me to get closer to her. As I did, she held my hand, and we both just stayed there waiting for Sasha. The wait seemed like an eternity. Then Sasha walked into the room.

"She is going to be fine; she just had a major shock and her system just reacted to it. She will be out of emergency in a few minutes, and she will be transferred to a room for observation. The doctor asked that we avoid giving her any other news that could set her back."

"Then I guess I should leave," I said. "I don't want my presence to hurt her even more. Sasha, could you please keep me posted? I will be at the station; you have both my cell and office numbers. There is still an attempted murder case involving a federal agent that has to be solved. The officers are still going to stay in place. Please let me know if you or Sarah need anything." And with those words, I left.

There were tears in my eyes; there was anger, and most of all, there were so many questions.

My day in the office was hard. I could not really think straight. I tried, but my mind was not on my work but at the hospital.

It was about 5:00 P.M. when I got a call from Sasha. She said that Sarah wanted to talk to all of us. She asked me to come to the hospital.

I told her that I would be there within the hour. I sat back on my chair, closed my eyes for a few minutes, then slowly got up, gave some instructions to the inspectors handling Fran's case, and left for the hospital.

This was not the trip that I wanted to do, but it was one I had to do.

I arrived the hospital and immediately went to Sarah's room. Sarah looked extremely fragile in the large bed. Fran was in a wheelchair next to the bed, holding her hand. Sasha was sitting by the foot of the bed, and there was another chair there. I guessed that one was for me.

Sarah greeted me and motioned for me to sit down. She took a long breath and started to tell her story.

"At the time of Fran's birth, Joe and I did not have any money, but we were happy, in our very tiny brownstone in New York. During my whole pregnancy, everyone asked me if I was going to have twins. My response was always the same, no. You see, at that time, sonograms were not routinely done for pregnancies unless there were really some problems."

She took a deep breath and looked at the two of us. Her eyes full of tears, she held tighter to Fran and then continued.

"Dr. Kevin O'Dell was recommended to us by a friend. She said he was a great doctor and did not charge a lot of money. So, we got in contact with him, and he became our doctor."

She looked at me with pain and tears in her eyes. And she continued.

"There were many times during the pregnancy that I asked him if I was expecting twins, and he said no. I told him that there were times I felt like there were two babies moving in my belly. He assured that there was only one baby. He said he would certainly if I was having twins, and no, I was not expecting twins. The day I delivered Fran, this new nurse I had never seen before was there. The doctor told me she was taking over for the regular nurse. And I believed him. I went into labor, and it felt like I had delivered a child, but the doctor said, no, and the regular nurse came in, so I continued to push. I did hear a child cry, and once again the doctor said it was in the other room. I felt so weak, and I believed him. Then a few minutes later, Fran came out crying. It was the best sound I had ever heard. She had some strong lungs, the doctor said. I held Fran in my arms, and a few days later, I was sent home. I never saw the first nurse again. When I got pregnant again, he was again my doctor. But that time, things seemed easier."

As she told her story, silent tears flowed down her cheeks.

I wanted to ask so many questions, but I refrained. I absorbed everything that I was being told. But was this the truth? My mother was dead, and so was my uncle. She could have known that, and to avoid problems with her daughter, she lied. Boy, am I being so cynical today. Her story was very possible.

If this really took place, my mother and uncle never thought we would ever meet. The story would have been kept a secret forever.

I got up from the chair, walked toward Sarah, gave her a kiss on her forehead, and left the room with a very heavy heart. If this story were true, then my mother stole me at birth and my uncle helped her. Did my father know about all this? What role did he play in all of this? So, once again, more questions.

I had taken a few personal days. This was not something I did often, but right now I needed time to process everything. Time to think and absorb all the information. In the last few weeks, I found out I had sister I did not know I had, and a twin sister at that. I found my biological mother who did not even know that I was born or that I even existed. My life in the last few weeks has been turned upside down, and I did not know how to get things upright again.

I sat on my couch. I had just opened a beer; Big Cat crawled on my lap. He never did that unless he could sense that there was something wrong.

There was a knock at my door. It had to be the Chinese food I had ordered. And I was right. I sat down, petted my cat, and ate my food in silence as I looked out my window.

About 8:00 P.M., I got a call from Claire. She asked if I was up to some company. I agreed, and she came by. Claire and I have been friends for many years. She was the assistant medical examiner in San Francisco when I was a homicide detective. Since then, she has been my friend, someone I could trust with everything. So, it did not surprise me when she came by. Half an hour later, she was knocking at my door.

"Hi there, I knew you wouldn't mind. But I knew that you needed a friend. So, here I am."

She came in, then sat down with me. We shared some food, had a few beers, and she heard my story. She could not believe it, but we had to find out the other side of the story. I knew in my heart that there must be an explanation for all of this.

"Question, do you still have some of your mother's and father's paper-work?" Claire asked.

"Yes, I do. It's all up in the attic," I said.

"Well then, first thing tomorrow, we are going through them. There has to be something in them that can help us find the truth. Also, we need to take a long look at your birth certificate. You do have the long form of it, right?"

I looked at her; as usual, she was ready to move forward. That was one of the many things I loved about her.

It was extremely late when we went to bed. We had spent the night talking about everything, and in the morning, we would be ready to tackle the task ahead of us.

About 10:00 A.M. in the morning, I awoke to the aroma of coffee. I had not slept this late in a long time.

"Hey, sleepyhead, time to get up. We have lots of work to do," she said loudly.

When I got to the kitchen, she had already served me my cup of coffee. We sat and planned our day. After I took a fast shower, we tackled the task ahead.

We spent all day looking in old boxes, both my mother's and my father's. But we were not able to find anything that could help us. It was about 7:00 P.M., and we were about to give up when out of the corner of my eye I saw an envelope that looked like the stationary my mother had. She loved to send letters and thank you notes.

I reached for it. It was my name on it in her handwriting. But the envelope seemed to have been opened.

I took out the seven-page letter in my mother's handwriting and read.

June 12, 1987

My dear daughter, there is so much I need to tell you, but I do not know where to start.

But I think the best thing to do is to start from the be-ginning.

I met your father in the summer of 1971. We knew right away that we were meant to be together. Within a few months, we got married. And we set out to make a family, but we were not successful.

At the time we met, your father was going to the police academy, and I was a nurse already.

You see, I came to California to visit some friends when I met your father and fell in love with him.

Not long after I met him, I found a job in the local hospital. Life with George was great, but he wanted a child so bad, and I could not give him one.

So, I contacted my brother, who was an OBGYN doctor and talked to him.

So, in September of 1975, I told George that I was going to visit my brother and left San Francisco for New York City. There, my brother ran a lot of tests, and he came with the same conclusions of the doctors in San Francisco. I was not going to be able to get pregnant. I was devastated. I so wanted to give your father a child.

I was about to return home when my brother said I should wait, that he had a plan, and he was sure it was going to work.

So, I sent your father a letter with a fake pregnancy test and told him I was going to stay in New York until I delivered. My brother had talked to him and told he recommended I should not fly and told him he would take good care of me.

I promised him I would keep him posted on how the pregnancy was coming along.

He said that he wished he could fly to New York, but he did not have the time to take to be with me.

It was at this time that my brother set about looking for a woman giving birth to twins who might fit the profile we needed. And we found one: she was Sarah Morris. She was expecting twins; she and her husband were struggling to make ends meet. He was a carpenter and was having a hard time finding a job.

My brother said that they looked like nice people, and that we would be doing them a favor.

And the plan was set; the first child to be born was mine, and the second hers. It did not matter what it was. We also agreed that we would register the child in New York and wait a few weeks before returning to San Francisco with the baby and the birth certificate that had my name and your father's name as parents.

Everything was set, and when you were born, you felt so good in my arms that there was no way I was going to give you up. And anyway, she was going to have another child. She would never know that she had two children.

My brother filed the birth certificate paperwork, and a few weeks later, when I got the certificate, I returned home.

There was no way anyone could find out. We were in California, and they were in New York. There was no way you could ever meet.

Time past so fast, and before we knew it, you were turning ten, and I thought this was the right time to write this letter.

I hope you get to read it when both your father and I are long gone. I also hope that you can forgive me. Finally, I truly hope that you are able to find your biological family.

Please forgive me. I hope they can also forgive me.

Your mother that loves you.
AnnMarie –

I put the letter down slowly. I felt like I had been punched in the gut. I cried; I was angry. I could not believe what I had just read.

Sarah was my biological mother; Fran was my sister. The life that I knew was all a lie. And he knew, my father knew. The letter was opened. He knew and kept the secret. What kind of cop was he? He lied and kept a stolen child as his.

After reading the letter, Claire looked at me. She could see the turmoil I was in.

"When did your mother pass?" she asked.

"A few days after this letter," I responded.

"Do you think your father knew?"

"My question is, why didn't he say something, even when he was dying? I don't understand," I said in an angry tone.

By the time we finished reading the letter, it was late. We ordered a pizza and had a beer as we waited for the pizza.

Many questions were answered: Why my mother never wanted to go and visit my uncle in New York City. Why she was so protective. I never understood, but now I do.

The pizza arrived, and a few beers later, we were both ready for bed. I knew the following day was not going to be easy.

By 8:00 A.M., I was ready. I had already called my office and talked to the inspector handling Fran's case. I had also spoken to Sasha and asked her how Fran and Sarah were doing. I told her about the letter and asked if she thought that both Sarah and Fran were ready to read it.

To my surprise, Sasha said that both Sarah and Fran were going home later that day. She asked me if I wanted to join them at the hospital and help her get them home.

I was incredibly happy with the invitation. I would bring the letter and hope that they would be able to read it and that we would set a plan to move forward.

Just before I headed out to the hospital, Claire said she was going to visit some other friends and that she would call me later. I asked her if she could lock up on her way out. And I left for the hospital.

CHAPTER 4
The Truth

I arrived the hospital just as Fran and Sarah were being released. I helped them get everything together and helped them get into Sasha's car.

I followed them. Fran and Sasha had an exceptionally beautiful townhouse in an exceptionally good area of San Francisco.

I helped Sasha get them both comfortable and then…

"I heard from Sasha that you found a letter from your mother that explains what happened. Can I read it, please?" Sarah said.

I hesitated, then Fran said, "Give it to me, I will read it."

Once again, I stalled, but Fran's eyes met mine, and I knew I had no choice.

It was at this time that Sasha came back into the room with two glasses of wine.

"Give her the letter; let's get this out in the open," she said as she handed me a glass of wine. She looked at Fran and said, "You don't get any; the doctor has not cleared you for alcohol, not even beer. I could get you a glass of water." Then all three of them laughed.

I handed Fran the letter, sat down, and listened to her read it. After she was finished, we all sat quietly for a few minutes, then I said, "Sarah, I am so sorry that all this took place. Your child was stolen; your time with that child was taken from you and the rest of your family. I am so sorry."

"I'm sorry too. I am sorry that we lost so much time together. I am sorry that I never got to the chance to cuddle you when you were sick or hurt yourself. I am sorry that you did not get the chance to grow up with your sister and your brother. That is what I am sorry about," she said.

There was so much I wanted to ask, but I knew she needed to rest; I could see in her face that she was tired. So, I did not ask anything, and I just enjoyed the time with these three women.

It was late when I left Fran's house. It had been a great evening.

The following morning as I had my coffee, I spoke with Claire on the phone. I told her all that had happened the night before. She listened, like she always did; and then she told me she had to get back to work. There was lot of work waiting her. I told her that I also needed to get to work, that we will speak later.

I got myself ready and went to the station. There were many cases I still had to take care of and especially the shooting of my sister. My sister! That sounded so strange.

As I settled in my office, I was advised that the FBI assistant special agent in charge was waiting for me. I had him come in. This was a conversation I needed to have.

"Hi, I am Lieutenant Sparks, great to meet you."

"Hi, I am Special Agent Joe Turner," he said as he showed me his credentials.

"Please sit down."

Special Agent Turner was about six, two, fair complexion, dark eyes (I would say that it felt like his eyes reflected his soul, a dark soul), salt-and-pepper hair, and was wearing a navy-blue suit with a royal blue tie.

I did not trust the FBI all that much. I have not had the best experience with them. But this time I really needed to find out what was going on with the woman who was now my sister.

"Special Agent Morris is the new special agent in charge of the local FBI office. She arrived at the office about six month ago. I do not understand why she was shot in your garage. I was aware that she wanted to meet you because she wanted to have a good working relationship between your office and ours," he said.

He then took a long look at me, and it was at that time realized that I looked so much like Fran.

"Wow, you two really look so much alike. If I did not better, I would swear you two were twins," he said.

I did not say anything about the fact that Fran and I were sisters. That was a story just for us, not a nosey FBI agent. And to be very sincere, I did not trust FBI agents.

He was not able to provide me any information about the cases Fran was working on. With the usual response, "a need to know," he danced around the subject. He asked if there were any cases that we at the SFPD were working on that might have led to her shooting. My response was "We will let you know" (two can play that game), and with that, the meeting was over. We shook hands, and he left my office.

I had a strange vibe about this guy. There was something about him I really did not like.

I asked Inspector Peterson to come to the office. She was a seasoned inspector, and she oversaw the case.

"Angie, what is going on with the garage shooting case?" I asked as she stood by the door.

Inspector Peterson was in her early forties, about five, eight; long, black hair; blue eyes; and a contagious smile.

"We found the car. It was abandoned in the Castro District. We got an anonymous report of where it was. The caller said that there was a black Mercedes Benz parked by a crack house. I found this strange, so we went to take a look, and yes, it was our car."

"Where is the car right now?"

"In the impound. The crime lab went through it with a fine comb and have not found anything. There are no fingerprints, no hair, no nothing. It felt like both the driver and the shooter were wearing hazmat suits to make sure there was no trace evidence left behind," she said.

"Then how do you know it was our car?" I asked.

"The tags. Vargas gave you the last four. When we got there; the tags were the same. Both the car and the tags were stolen the day prior to the shooting. Both the tags and the car were reported stolen on the day of the shooting. And one more thing, there were some small splatters of blood that matched that of Agent Morris. It confirms that this was the car used in the shooting," she stated.

"Okay, thanks. Please find something that can lead us to the shooter. I have the chief, the mayor, and now DC breathing down my neck to solve this."

As she was about to leave, she looked at me and said:

"You do understand that you two look alike, and that maybe she was not the target. Maybe you were. During your career, you've helped put away a lot of bad guys. Maybe one with a grudge shot her thinking it was you. Even Officer Vargas thought it was you," she said.

"That was one of my first thought. I am looking at some of my hate mail. I will be making a list and giving it to you so you can check them out."

I spent the rest of the day going through a lot of hate mail and emails and reviewing old cases. I had not realized how many people hated me.

About 6:00 P.M., I got a call from Fran asking me if I liked beer and pizza. I was glad to hear from her, and my answer to her question was an enthusiastic YES.

So, I headed to their house. I was looking forward to spending more time with them. With the mother and sister I never knew I had.

I arrived the house and was received with warmth. It was so great to sit down and have good pizza and beer.

It was about 8:00 P.M. when the shooting started. Fran and I were sitting in the living room talking; Sasha had gone to help Sarah in the kitchen.

The sound of bullets is clearly distinguishable, especially the sound of a large caliber gun. Both Fran and I hit the floor. The shooting continued for several seconds. When it was all over, both of us, at the same time, asked if everyone was okay. The answer was in the affirmative.

I immediately called it in; Fran went outside to look. Both her car and mine were riddled with bullets. There was no damage to the house, but whoever did this either wanted to send a message or create confusion about who the intended victim was.

Within minutes, CSI personnel were on scene, as well as Inspector Peterson, her partner, and maybe half of the SFPD. The cars were towed to the impound, and Peterson let me use her car, and she returned to the station in a black and white.

After making sure that Fran and her family were all right, I returned to the station. What was all this shooting about? Who was it aimed at, me or Fran? If it was me, why? If it was her, again why? I had to find out what was going on before someone else got hurt.

CHAPTER 5
SOLVING THE CRIME

As the investigation continued in both shootings, I invited Fran to my apartment. It was the same two-bedroom apartment I had been living in for ages. I just did not want to give it up.

Fran arrived about 6:00 P.M. Sasha had dropped her off and told me to call her when Fran was ready to go home. Fran was still convalescing from her wounds and was not allowed to drive. In addition, her car was still in the impound being analyzed. So, they had a rental.

I had ordered some Chinese food. Let it be known that I never said I was a good cook, better still, any kind of cook.

We sat and talked about everything: our lives, our childhood, dating, marriage, everything. I always wanted a sister, but I never thought I would find her so late in my life.

As the sun started to come up, we realized we had spent the whole night together, talking and getting to know each other.

"I have about four texts from Sasha. She wants to know if she needs to come and get you," I said.

"I have more, but I answered her that we were okay. She's just worried," she said.

As I served her a cup of coffee, she asked, "Have you found out anything about the attempts against us?"

"Nothing more than what I told you earlier. At first I thought the attempt was against me, and I still think that. I think they confused you with me, and the shooting at your house just seemed strange. Were they after you or me?"

"I think someone is playing with us. Someone is trying to distract us, someone who knows we look alike. There is something going on, and they are trying to keep us busy chasing small leads," she said.

"Your shooting was not nothing. You could have died."

"I know. So, let's put this puzzle together. We need to solve this."

For the next few hours, we tried to put the pieces of the puzzle together. Who knew that she was going to be at my office that particular day?

There were no attempts against Fran in the hospital because there were two officers posted at her door 24/7. But there was an attempt when we were both together. It was a very lame attempt, no one got hurt, but there was an attempt. But who was it intended for?

Once again, so many question and so few answers.

At about 9:00 A.M., Peterson arrived with the case file. She looked at both of us, and I could see that she had tons of questions, but she made no comments, and I did not provide any answers.

We spent the rest of the day going through the case. It all seemed to lead us to a dead end, until Peterson said, "I think this is a ruse. You see, I Googled you both, and both of you have had very solid careers. Both of you have been highly decorated. Whoever is behind this wants to keep you both chasing your tails. This is someone close to one of you, someone either in the FBI or in the department."

"Let's take a look at the first shooting. Fran, who knew you were coming to my office?" I asked.

"My assistant. He was the one who urged me to go. He said that in the past, there had been some bad blood between our offices and maybe it might be good to mend fences. I agreed, but before I went, I Googled you. I did see our resemblance, but I put it aside at the time," she said.

"So, you knew who I was when you saw me in the hospital?" I asked.

"Yes, but it was so different seeing you in person. Did you Google me?" she said.

"Yes, I did, and was surprised with the resemblance," I said.

"Let's put this together. Your assistant knew you were coming to my office. I bet you he Googled us the same way we Googled each other. He was able to see the resemblance. And at the same time, Officer Vargas was in the garage at the exact time of the shooting," I said.

"My question is, what was Vargas doing in the garage at that time? Wasn't he supposed to be on patrol?" Peterson asked.

"There has to be a connection between Vargas and Turner. Turner was the only one who knew when I was going to your office, and I would bet Vargas was there waiting to give the signal," Fran said.

"We are leaping into conclusions here with no proof," I said. "If we are going to make the case, we have to make sure we are working with facts. Is there is a connection between Vargas and Turner?"

"I don't know, Jane. There is something very fishy here. Let's recap. One, I tell my assistant agent that I am going to your office after his insistence that I should. Then Officer Vargas is waiting for me to show up just as the car with the shooter approaches and shoot," she said.

"Peterson, did you get tapes from the garage level where the shooting took place?"

"No, Lieutenant, all the cameras in that level were disable by a laser," Peterson responded.

"All the cameras; so there is no way we can tell at what time the black Mercedes enter the garage. Do you know who let that car in?"

"Yes, and Officer Voytogi. I checked it out, and we don't have any officer by that name in the force," Peterson responded.

"Voytogi, that is a very strange name," Fran said.

"Wait a minute, what if the V is a U, and the name is Uoytogi. Or maybe, "I got you," I said.

"That makes sense. If they were trying to distract us in a wild goose chase, that makes lots of sense." Fran said.

"We need to talk to Vargas again, have him meet us at the station. I think I need to have a long talk with him."

Peterson called the station to make the arrangements, to discover that Vargas was not at work that day; he had not shown up for work the past few days, and he has not even called in. Peterson requested a squad car go to his house and do a wellness check. And said that she and the lieutenant would be there soon.

Fran said she wanted to go. But I told her she needed to stay. She was still recovering from her injuries, and I was sure the doctor hard not cleared her for duty. "I am calling Sasha to come and pick you up."

As I was about to reach for the phone to call Sasha to come and pick her, Fran took the phone from my hand and in an extraordinarily strong voice said: "I am going with you, either in your car or I will find some other way. But I am going. This one is personal."

I paused for a second and realized that this woman was not going to follow my orders and that it was best for her to go with me so I could keep an eye on her.

"Well, let's go," I said.

Shortly after, all three of us were at Vargas's house. There had been no answer to knocking on the door. The officers who had arrived earlier had looked around but could not see anything.

As both Fran and I approached the house, there was total silence. One officer stared at us with complete surprise. The others tried in vain not to look. I introduced Fran, and after getting an update, I ordered them to break open the door.

As we walked in, we could smell that something was not good. Then we found Vargas. He seemed to have been dead for a few days. I called for the medical examiner and CSI.

When Vargas's house was processed, it was discovered that it had been wiped clean. There was no sign of a struggle, no sign it was a suicide. There was nothing, except for one small piece of paper he was holding in his hand. It had the date of the first shooting and a phone number.

"I know this number," Fran said, and she dialed it. It went straight to the voicemail of Assistant Agent Turner.

"I guess it's time to pay Agent Turner a visit."

Fran obtained Agent Turner's address, and we headed that way. Turner lived in an apartment in a good part of town. Peterson, Fran, and I identified ourselves, and Fran told the apartment manager that she was his boss and that we wanted to do a wellness check. The manager seemed a bit confused but still went with us and opened the door of the apartment after knocking several times.

And once again, in the middle of the floor was the body of Turner, shot the same way as Vargas. Once again, the apartment was wiped clean. Again, there was nothing.

Both Turner's apartment and Vargas's house were totally wiped clean. Not even their fingerprints were found. There was nothing at all but two very immaculate places.

After the apartment was processed, the body was removed. The lack of any evidence was staggering.

After hours of processing the crime scene, Fran and I headed to the FBI office to search Turner's desk.

His desk was immaculate, not a single piece of paper out of place. His files were simply perfect with every single note and FBI form attached to each one. There was nothing that could tell us if there was a connection to Vargas.

Then, at the very back of the middle drawer of his desk, Fran found a small piece of paper. It had Vargas's name, phone number, and address.

"Here is the connection between these two guys. But who wanted them dead? This was just too easy. Each man had the other's phone number just visible enough to make us wonder," Fran said.

I had to agree with her. This was just too easy. We needed a fall guy, and we got two, one from each department. This was the time to really dig deeper. And just before I could say anything, Peterson said, "I will be looking at their finances and also any investigations where they might have connected. Any investigation that they could have been working on. Anything that could tie them together."

"I guess this is a case where both the FBI and the SFPD will have to work together. I hope you guys at the SFPD are willing to play ball," Fran said with a very wicked smile.

"Keep us both posted on anything you find, Peterson," I said.

Turning to Fran, I said, "Let me take you home before Sasha and Sarah think I have kidnapped you."

"You mean our mother," she said.

That statement felt so strange. Until a few weeks ago, I did not know that I had a sister and, least of all, another mother. This was going to take some getting used to.

Fran turned to me; she saw my hesitation, and she said, "We have to learn to be sisters. I know that will be something Mom would like. She already loves you and wants to know you better. Also, you are going to have to meet Tommy, his wife and two children."

I had forgotten. Now not only did I have a new mother and sister, but also a brother, two sisters-in-law, and a niece and a nephew. My family has grown so much in just a few weeks.

But what was still at the forefront of my mind was, Who was behind the assault on us? I knew that we had to be vigilant, but that was not going to stop me from enjoying my new family.

Fran and I left the FBI office. We were talking about so many things. We even laughed and teased one another. I guess this was an FBI agent I might have to trust.

This was going to be the end, at least for now.

CHAPTER 6
What Do We Know?

It has been about six months since Fran got shot and we found out we were sisters. But the case is now a cold case. We still can't find the connection between Turner and Vargas. We have no idea why Fran was shot.

This case might be a cold case to the SFPD, but not for me. I need answers to my questions, and I will get the answers. I know somewhere out there is a connection to all this, and I will find it. But as of right now, I am enjoying my newfound family.

As Fran and I sat on her porch, enjoying the San Francisco afternoon breeze, Fran looked at me and said, "We need to take a close look at the case. I know that for the SFPD, it's a cold case but not for the FBI. One of our agents was shot and another was killed."

"I agree with you," I said.

"So where do we start?" she asked in a rhetorical way.

"We go back to the beginning: you getting shot," I said. "You said that only Turner knew that you were going to my office. So, what did he have to gain if you got shot and killed?"

"I don't think it had to do with him becoming the new senior special agent in charge. He could get that promotion and move to another place," she said. "And we haven't found a single connection between Vargas and Turner."

I immersed myself in my thoughts. This is a bad habit I have when I really need to find answers, and this time was no different. Fran was right. We checked their finances; they did not bank at the same bank. One thing I did find interesting was the fact that Vargas was getting a deposit on the fifteenth of every month to his account of fifteen thousand dollars for the last two years, from a Cayman Islands bank. However, the account could not be traced. Turner was getting the same amount, not on the fifteenth, but on the first of the month from a totally different account from a different bank in the Cayman Islands. Both accounts were totally hard to trace and even more difficult to get a warrant. These looked that payroll payments. But what were they getting paid for? And who was their boss?

With a cough, Fran got me out of myself and back to the moment. I had shared this info with her in the hope that the FBI could get the info on the banks, but at this time, she had not been able to get anything.

"Sis, we need to go back to the beginning. Someone ordered my shooting, and even though I was in the hospital for a few weeks, the injury was not deadly. If they wanted to kill me, they had the opportunity and the means, and they did not do it. My shooting was a distraction," Fran said.

"My question is still the same, Why? We did not know each other at that time, and we did not know we were sisters. What would they gain by shooting you and not killing you?" I wondered.

"Distraction, confusion. We might not have known we were sisters, but they might have," she said.

"Explain?" I asked.

"Turner was very insistent to the fact that I should go and meet with you on that day. I told him I had lots of work to do and that I would go some other day. But he would not take no for an answer, so I made the call to tell your office that I was going to meet with you. I was expecting that the person who answered would tell me that you were too busy, and if my visit was not related to a particular case, that I might need to go another day. But that did not happen. So, I left for your office," Fran said.

"Do you remember who answered the phone?" I asked.

"It was a guy, and he did not give me his name. He asked at what time I was going to be there and said he would tell you," Fran said.

"So, going back to the original question, how did they know we were sisters?" I asked.

"The same way we found out: DNA," she said.

"But how?" I asked.

"You must not read a lot of mystery detective stories. They took the DNA from either your coffee cup, a drink, or your hairbrush from your house. The same with me. Remember, both men had many ways to get into our homes and get what they needed. If not them, the people they were working for."

She was right. I did not read a lot of crime mystery stories; I am more of a sci-fi type of reader. But I digress. We must start at the very beginning: who shot Fran Morris, and why?

"You said we must go back to the beginning. I have a question for you, which is a question that many have asked, How can an FBI agent afford such a beautiful house in such an exclusive area of San Francisco?"

Fran laughed and said, "You do know I am married, right?" and she looked at me in a very mischievous look. "Once again, you really do not read a lot of mystery detective stories. Do me a favor, go in your phone and Google Sasha Dean," she said with a smile. "As you can see, my wife is an incredibly famous mystery detective writer. She used to be the medical examiner for the State of New York. Then she decided to become a writer, and she used the knowledge she obtained from her previous work for her novels and became very, very famous and rich," she said with a smile.

"Sorry, but I wanted to get things out in the open. I hate surprises," I said.

"I did tell you how we met, right? I was chasing a suspect down East 63rd Street. I was focused on the chase, did not see where I was going, and slammed right into her. She fell to the ground. I apologized but kept going. I spilled her coffee on her, and she was not a happy camper. A few days later, she was at my office demanding to speak to me and demanding that I pay for her dry cleaning. I once again apologized. We established a friendship. One thing led to another, and we got married, and here we are. Does that truly answer your questions?" she said with a laugh.

"I am sorry," I said, feeling very stupid.

"Now, can we get back to the beginning?" she asked.

"So, what do we know: that they were able to get our DNA and that they figured out that we were sisters. We also know that both Turner and Vargas were paid from accounts in the Cayman Islands. That is not a lot," I said.

"We really don't have a lot," she looked at me and said.

Once again there was silence as we both drank some beer and looked out into the night.

CHAPTER 7
THE FIRST GOOD LEAD

It seemed that this case was definitely going the wrong way. I felt like no matter that what we did, it led nowhere. There were no leads at all, and time was ticking away. At least on that front.

For the rest, my relationship with my sister and her wife was growing, and yes, I started to read Sasha's books. She really is a great writer.

I sat at my desk going through a case. This is the part of my job I hate the most. I love to be out on the streets solving cases. But now, I sit here and read cases before we send them to the district attorney's office. While I was reading, Inspector Peterson knocked on my door.

"Can I come in?" she asked.

"Sure, what's up?" I said.

"I think I have a lead on the Fran Morris case," she said.

I enthusiastically waved her in. "What do you have for me?" I asked.

"Some months back I lost contact with one of my CIs. Yesterday, I got a call from him. He told me he had been in the hospital because he had been shot. The shooter left him for dead, but he was taken to the hospital and he slowly recovered," she said.

"Did you get anything from him?" I asked.

"More than what I was expecting. He told me that he had tried to contact me but could not. So, he had approached an officer and asked the officer if he knew me. The officer said he did, and my CI asked him to relay to me that he had heard there was a new trafficking ring in the San Francisco area. He was not sure what the ring was trafficking, but as soon as he knew, he would contact me," she said.

"So, what did he tell when you were able to see him yesterday?" I asked.

"After he explained to me what had happened to him, I was able to show him a few photos of officers, and I included the one of Vargas. Without hesitation, he pointed Vargas out. He also told me that the person that shot him had a military type of tattoo on his right wrist," she said.

"So, the shooting of your CI and Fran's shooting are related. Is that what you are trying to say?" I asked.

"Yes, but we have no idea what this new trafficking ring is bringing into the city. Drugs, women, knock-off designer clothing, we really don't know," she said.

"That is true, but at least we have an idea what we're looking for. A new smuggling ring," I stated.

"But how does this connect to your sister?" she asked.

"The FBI works cases of trafficking in connection with the DEA and local police. But I don't think she had any knowledge of this. She would have told me. I believe the info got to Turner's desk via Vargas, and that is what cause their deaths. The puppet master felt his puppets were not doing their job and had them killed," I said. "Anything else?" I asked.

"No. nothing, I will keep you posted," she said and left my office.

As soon as Peterson left my office, I called Fran at her office and asked her if she had heard anything about a new trafficking ring in the San Francisco area or if it was a "need to know" thing. She laughed and said that she had not heard anything about that and she would investigate it.

After I hung up, I set out to investigate things on my own. There was a new trafficking ring in my city, and I needed to find out who was behind it and what they were doing in my city.

I set a meeting with the vice unit and drug unit lieutenants regarding this possible new trafficking ring. After a long meeting with them, I was back to square one. No one had heard of this new trafficking ring. Could this be just a ruse to get me off the trail? It felt like every day that passed, the case got colder. It might be getting colder, but I am not going to give up. I still have this gut feeling that there is something really behind all this, and I am as determined as the first day to find out what and who it is.

CHAPTER 8
FAMILY TIME

It had been several weeks since I had spoken with Fran. In a very strange way, I needed that contact with her. Being an only child, in a family where my dad was a cop and my mother a nurse, I spent many times alone. Now, at this time in my life, having a sister was a great gift.

It was Friday night, and what better way to spend the evening than with family and friends. First, I called Fran to see if she and Sasha wanted to come over for dinner. It is well understood that I do not cook, so it would be a takeout dinner, and a surprise one. Fran accepted the invitation, and we set the time for 7:30. That would give me time to go and pick up our dinner.

After talking to Fran, I called Claire. She has been a long time and dear friend. She recently lost her husband and a child in a tragic car accident and I was recovering from the trauma of a divorce.

"Hi Claire, two questions: would you like to join Fran, Sasha, and I for dinner at my apartment?" I asked.

"Sure, what are you getting?" she said.

"Have you heard about Puerto Rican food?" I asked.

"Yes, I love it," she said.

"Is it close to Mexican food?" I asked.

"No, nothing like that. It is seasoned different and is very tasty. I really like it. Why do you ask?" she said.

"It seems Fran likes it," I said.

"Of course, being from New York City. There is a large Puerto Rican population, but there is a growing population of Puerto Ricans here in San Francisco. I am texting you the name of one of the best Puerto Rican restaurants in town. Their specialty is 'mofongo.' I know you will like it after you try it," she said, extremely excited.

"Mofongo? That sounds strange, but to please you and my sister, I will try it. What else should I get?" I asked.

She rattled of a list of things I should order and agreed to be at my house a little before 7:30 to help me set up the food. She would also be bringing some wine. Everything seemed to be going great for this evening, and I was looking forward to a great night with family and friends.

Then, as I was getting ready to leave my office, the thought of Tom came to my mind. This was something I had not had in a while. My divorce from Tom became formal about a year ago, about the time I finally made it to lieutenant. We had been married for almost ten years. He always wanted me to be behind a desk. He was worried that I could get killed in the line of duty and he did not want to be that husband waiting for news. This was ironic, considering that he traveled constantly due to his business. So for much of our time together, I could say I was single.

Tom is a good man. He makes a good friend, and that was what our relationship was mostly about, being friends more than husband and wife. But enough about Tom. Let's get this night started.

I went to pick up the food. It really smelled great. A few minutes after I got home, Claire arrived, and shortly after that, Fran and Sasha arrived.

As Fran and Sasha entered, I told them I had a surprise for them. We were having Puerto Rican food. The surprise on Fran's face was great. She had mentioned to me some time back that she loved Puerto Rican food. To my surprise, I had chosen for dinner everything she liked. Yes, this was going to be a great evening.

As we were sitting at the table to enjoy our food, there was a knock on the door. Fran went to get it.

"Hi, gorgeous," the male voice said and proceeded to kiss her.

"I think you got the wrong person," she said.

"Jane, I think there is someone here at the door looking for you," she said.

As I approached the door, I saw Tom. This was a totally unexpected visit. I had not seen Tom for quite a while, and I had no idea he was going to stop by tonight.

"Oh, hi Tom, please come in. Let me introduce you to my sister Fran. Fran, this is Tom, my ex-husband," I said.

Tom was completely surprised. I told him all about how we found out we were sisters, and we invited him to stay and have dinner with us. He was happy with the idea and joined us.

Time passed amazingly fast, and before we all realized it, it was almost midnight. Fran, Sasha, and Claire said good night and left. Tom, on the other hand, stayed. We continued our conversation until well into the morning. Tom left my apartment about 3:00 A.M. All in all, it was a great evening.

CHAPTER 9
THE FIRST BIG BREAK

It was late Monday afternoon when I got a call from Fran at my office. She told me she believed that she had stumbled over something that might be a lead to our smuggling case.

"What do you know about horses and horse raising?" she asked.

"Something, I used to be in the SFPD Mounted Police," I said

"That is great to know. How about if you stop by my office first thing tomorrow morning? I have something remarkably interesting to share with you," she said.

"How about if I go over there now, I have no patience and I hate to wait." I replied.

"No problem, I will see you in a few," she said.

The 5:00 P.M. traffic in San Francisco is murder. It took me about an hour to get the federal building, and after clearing security, I went straight Fran's office.

"So, sis, enlighten me," I said.

"I'm sure you know that horse racing is part of the drug trafficking culture," she said.

"No, I did not know that, but where are you going with this?" I asked.

"I was looking through one of Turner's cases before I reassigned it to another agent when I found attached to the folder a list of horses and racetracks, then the words 'Mill Valley,' 'Vallejo,' 'delivery,' and 'race,' These words were highlighted." She continued, "I took a look at the areas he mentioned and found out that there is a Sunset Racetrack in Vallejo. It is not a very well-known racetrack, but it is an established racetrack. I also found Monroe Stables and Training in Mill Valley, a horse training ranch which is, again, in a not very well-known place," she said.

"I still don't understand where you are going with this," I said.

"After I found this paper, I did some research. Did you know that in a horse smuggling case in Austin, Texas, one of the witnesses stated that quarter horse racing is ingrained in the drug trafficking culture in Northern Mexico and South Texas. In a 2008 federal case, a US citizen and a businessman was accused of helping a drug cartel launder money through horse racing. According to the indictment, the businessman owned more than twenty horses when he started working for the gang," she continued as she provided me with newspaper articles and federal court paperwork. "The US citizen owned horses on both sides of the border. This made him an important figure in a scheme to launder millions through the US horse racing industry."

"So, you believe that this is the trafficking we had heard about?" I asked.

"Yes, I really do. Who would suspect a horse trainer and a racetrack of smuggling and laundering cartel money? But there is more. The scheme is when a horse performed well, the US citizen would arrange a sham sale with his brother who owned a horse ranch. The first horse to win a race was in 2009, so the brothers had their straw buyer pretend to buy the horse for thirty grand. The US citizen could show the IRS the thirty grand and that the horse had won half a million dollars so it all looked clean," she stated.

I was stunned. I would have never thought of this, but Fran was thorough. She continued.

"In the indictment, prosecutors allege that the Texas businessman was with the cartel and bought horses that were later transferred to another of their front men in the US."

She looked at me with an expression as if to say, "I'm not done," so I sat down, got comfortable in my chair, took the coffee she was offering, and continued to be educated about horse trafficking.

"It was discovered that the cartel hid millions through a horse farm. In 2011, a particular quarter horse farm in Oklahoma was booming with business—even as the recession was taking a toll on the usually lucrative industry. As I kept researching this, I found out that, according to federal investigators, what seemed like a ranch filled with the top mares was actually a front for a multimillion-dollar money-laundering scheme orchestrated by one of the most dangerous Mexican drug cartels." She continued, "There were multiple indictments and convictions from this case. The cartel really thought that the quarter horse racing industry was a great place to run this scheme and stay under the radar from US law enforcement."

I was amazed at her research ability regarding this. It all started with a piece of paper with a few words scribbled on it and it was leading to a possible scheme of horse trafficking and money laundering.

This really was a totally interesting and strange possible case, if this was what was happening here.

But Fran was not done with her presentation. According to Fran, the lead investigator on the case had immersed himself in the case for years. This all started with a tip from an informant in 2010, and it concluded with convictions in 2011.

"Wow, this is very interesting, but again, where is this all leading?" I asked.

"I understand that you're skeptical about this but think about it. This is just a great way to smuggle horses into the country, race them, and use them for money laundering. Then once they have served their purpose here in the Bay Area, they can be sold to someone somewhere and the horse will have his/her name changed and still make them more money," she said.

"If you put it that way, it is a great scheme. No one would think of horse racing to launder drug money. But proceeding with this is not going to be easy. We need to find the right connection within the horse training and racing business," I said.

"You're right, but didn't you just say that you were part of the SFPD Mounted Police? You must have developed some kind of connection. I also think this is a very interesting theory. Don't you think so?" she said.

"It's as good as anything we have right now. I will contact some of my CIs to see if they know anything about a big sale of imported horses from Mexico. You keep digging through your federal cases and see what you can come up with," I said as I got up from my chair.

It was late when I left her office. As I walked toward my car, I could feel someone was following me. This did not feel good. We had already had one of us shot; we did not want the other one also shot. The person following me moved fast, and before I knew it, he was on me. He was in a full hazmat suit, and before I could get to my gun, he stabbed me. As I dropped to the ground, I heard him say, "This is just a warning, stay out of it, or you could end up six feet under."

As I was dropping to the ground and he was speaking, I was able to get my gun out, and I shot him in the leg. This surprised him, and he stabbed me again. This time I felt like I was a goner. And this time, I could not shoot him again. In the midst of all this, I was able to see the military tattoo on his right wrist as I passed out. The next thing I remember was waking up in a hospital bed, with Fran by my side. It was so strange to see my face staring back at me, but this time we both knew about the other. But what we did not know was who was behind all of this.

"How are you doing?" she asked with a worried look on her face.

"In pain, but alive. How did I get here?" I asked.

"I found you. You somehow managed to FaceTime me, and I found you, called the paramedics, and we got you here. I contacted Inspector Peterson, and now it is you who has two officers at your door," she said.

"Thanks very much," I said.

"How about if you rest and we can talk about all this later? Tom is on his way, and so is Claire. I will stay with you until they get here. I do not want you to be alone at any time," she said with a smile.

I closed my eyes. I felt exhausted, angry, and very frustrated, but I knew that I had to rest to make sure I got better and found the person who was responsible for all this.

"This story is not over," I said to myself as I closed my eyes.

CHAPTER 10
IN PLAIN SIGHT

It had been a few weeks since my stabbing, something that I found interesting. Why the stabbing? That was close and personal. I knew he wanted to make a point, but that close, I wondered.

As I sat in my apartment still waiting to be cleared for work from the doctors, I was going through in my mind about the events leading to my stabbing. He was moving fast; it felt like he was there by the time I was able to turn around.

As I pondered about it all, there was a knock on my door. When I went to open it, there was Fran and Inspector Peterson.

"Well, you are looking better," Fran said with a smile, "I guess with all that mothering you were getting, you were definitely going to get better soon," she continued with a wicked smile as they both entered the apartment.

"Yes. You know, I missed my mother; she was a beautiful and caring woman. I know what she and my uncle did was unspeakable, but, to me, she was a great mother. And now, knowing my real mother and letting her take care of me was strange in a nice way. I wondered many times how it would have been if I had been able to grow up with you and Tommy. But that is something we will never know, so I am planning to take advantage of every moment I can with her," I said.

Fran went straight to the kitchen and served herself and Peterson some coffee, then we all sat down in my living room to talk.

"I know you're still not cleared for duty, but I have a few questions. Do you remember anything else about the stabbing?" she asked.

"As a matter of fact, I was just thinking about that when you guys came in. Even though he was wearing a full hazmat suit, mask, and all, I was able to see his eyes. They were blue and cold. He may have been a white guy. He was tall, and he seemed to be extraordinarily strong. But I gave all this information to you before," I said as I looked at Peterson.

"Yes, I know," she said. "But we wanted to make sure if you might have remembered something else."

"Okay, I am going to FaceTime Claire. There was something she wanted to tell you," Fran said as she dialed Claire's phone and got her on.

"Hi there, how are you doing?" Claire asked.

"Not bad, ready to go back to work. Peterson said that you have come up with something," I said.

"I am sending you a photo of a tattoo that I found on a John Doe that was brought in earlier this morning. Does it look like the one your attacker had?" she asked.

I opened the photo on my phone, and there it was, the same tattoo that I had seen the night of my stabbing. I looked up at both Fran and Peterson, then I said, "Claire, there is no doubt in my mind that is the same tattoo. But you said it was on a body found earlier today?" I said.

"Well, this man has been dead for about seventy-two hours. He was found in the Castro District. He has been shot and stabbed; can you say overkill? Then his tongue was cut out. That happened after he was dead. I think that part was more of a message to others," Claire said.

"There was no way to run his prints. They were burned off with acid," Peterson said.

"So, we're back to square one," I said, very frustrated.

"Maybe not," Peterson said. "Remember that young equestrian you helped some years back, the one that had her horse stolen."

"Yes, I do, but that was sometime back. That was even before I became an inspector. Why?" I asked.

"Well, she called and asked for you about three days ago. The call was transferred to me. She said she needed to talk to you, that it was urgent. I told her that you were on medical leave and that I would pass on the message. She gave me a phone number and said to tell you it was particularly important."

I picked up my phone and called her right away. I put my phone on speaker so the others could hear the conversation. As she answered the phone, I could hear that she was in some kind of horse facility.

I had met Dorothy some years back, when she was a young girl with dreams of becoming an Olympic equestrian. A bad fall from her horse during practice cut that dream short, but we kept in touch through the years. Then one day she called me. She was crying and told me her horse had gone missing. We contacted animal protection and looked everywhere and finally found him; he had been shot. We could not understand why someone would do something like that. After that, we still kept in touch. She had found work at one of the local racetracks and was working as a stable hand. Her dreams of being an Olympic equestrian were gone, and so were her dreams of being a jockey. So, she decided that she wanted to keep working with horses and became a stable hand.

"Hi Dorothy, I was told you needed to talk to me urgently. What is going on?" I asked.

"Yes, remember when you said some time back that if I saw something strange to call you?" she said, then she continued, "Well, I know this is not related to your work, but there are some really strange people wandering around here at the Monroe Stables and Training where I work. I do not like them. They seem very sinister, and they've been nosing all around. Then right after they came, two new horses were brought to the stables. No one was allowed to get near them, just one particular trainer and helper. When I tried to get closer to the horses, I was told to stay away and mind my own business if I knew what was good for me. I thought I should call you. Maybe it's nothing, but I wanted to pass on my concerns," she said.

"Thank you for the information. Can you describe the men you saw?" I asked.

"Yes, one was tall, white, with cold blue eyes. He had some kind of tattoo on his right wrist. He looked very menacing. The other guy was shorter, dark hair, and eyes and not as menacing as the other guy. They both spoke Spanish. I couldn't get close enough to hear all that much, but they were talking about a race and that they needed to make sure they won it," she said.

"When did this all take place?" I asked.

"About three weeks ago. I called you right away, and they told me you were on medical leave. Then I tried again and talked to an Inspector Peterson who told me you were still on medical leave and I told her to tell you that I had called."

"When did you speak to Peterson?" I asked.

"I want to say about three days ago. She said she would pass on the message. I don't know if there is anything thing here, but I thought I would let you know," she said.

"Thank you for the information. Please stay safe and keep me informed of anything else you feel is strange at the stable," I said and ended the conversation.

We all looked at each other. The pieces of the puzzle might be coming together. Maybe Fran was right; this whole smuggling ring has to do with horses and money laundering.

I went to get more coffee as I thought out loud.

"Turner and Vargas were the leaks to the FBI and the SFPD. They were supposed to keep the puppeteer informed of any activity regarding horse smuggling and horse racing."

"But why shoot me?" Fran asked. Then she said, "Turner knew that I had no idea what was going on. If I did, I would have talked to him about it."

"That is right, but your shooting was a ruse. It was meant to keep us distracted while they smuggled in the horses. They knew that we would be involved in finding out about our relationship and would not be paying attention to the smuggling," I said.

"Okay, I buy that," Peterson said. "But why killed Turner and Vargas?" she asked.

"Simple: they served their purpose; they were a liability, so they had to go," Fran said.

"And they went after me as another form of distraction. But this time I was supposed to die. When they found out that I had shot their man and I was still alive, then he became a liability," I said.

"But who is that top connection between the cartel and the FBI and SFPD?" I asked. "It has to be someone very high up, someone that no one would ever suspect."

"But who?" Fran asked, and the question hung there for a few minutes.

"Did you guys know that the chief is an avid horse aficionado?" Peterson said.

"No, I did not, but how do you know?" I asked.

"When you were gone, she called me to her office and was asking how you were doing. That was when I saw all her horse memorabilia. I asked her about it, and she said she had always been a horse racing fan," she said.

"Okay, this is getting interesting," Fran said.

"Yes, but we just cannot be assuming that the chief of the SFPD is involved in horse trafficking. We have to be a hundred percent sure," I said.

"Well, the first thing we have to do is find the link between Turner, Vargas, the tattoo guy, and the chief. Then comes the hard part, establishing the case against her. And that, my friends, is not going to be easy. She is very well connected and well-liked by the mayor and other city officials," Fran said.

"If we haven't found the connection between Turner and Vargas as of now, how you think we are going to find the connection between all of them now?" I asked.

Then I thought about it. I would pay a visit to the chief as soon as I was reinstated. I would take a close look at her office and the horse racing memorabilia. Maybe the clue is in those trophies and memorabilia.

A few days had gone by, and I finally got my letter of reinstatement. I was cleared for duty. My first order of business was to visit the chief and thank her for the beautiful flowers she had sent to the hospital.

The chief was an incredibly beautiful woman. She was tall, long black hair that she wore in a bun, penetrating dark eyes, and she looked like she was ready to stroll down a Paris runway.

As I was escorted into her office by her assistant, I was able to see a large number of photos of horses on her wall, but the one that attracted me the most was that of a young man in uniform, and the man right next to him was a young Vargas, and the other one was a young Turner.

"I see you are a fan of horse racing," I said as I sat down.

"Yes, my husband and I loved horses. That was a great passion of his," she said, "and I believe it is a great passion of yours also," she added.

"What do you mean?" I asked.

"Weren't you part of the SFPD Mounted Police?" she said.

"That is right," I said as I got up to look at some of the photos on her wall.

"I am glad to see you are doing better," she said as she joined me.

"Yes and thank you so much for that beautiful tulip bouquet you sent to hospital. How did you know I liked tulips?" I asked.

"You do not get to become chief of police without knowing something about your fellow officers," she said, then added, "You didn't just come here to thank me, did you?"

"Yes, I did. I found the detail of the flowers very touching, and I wanted to thank you in person," I said.

"That was very thoughtful of you. Is there anything you want to tell me?" she asked.

"No, that was it. Once again thank you, and please take care," I said as I left the office.

I went straight to my office, just a few floors down. Then I contacted Fran and told her about what I had seen. The connection between Turner and Vargas was the army. The connection between our tattooed man was also the army. It seemed, I told her, that the chief's son or younger brother was with Vargas and Turner in the army at the same time and at the same time as our mystery killer.

Our conversation lasted a few minutes, and she agreed to run Turner's military record. I thought that would be the best thing. I did not want to raise any red flags so soon after leaving the chief's office.

But, to my surprise, I did not have to wait very long to find out the connection between them all.

As I was going home that night, I could see a car following me. It seemed like an undercover car, but I could not be all that sure. I went through some simple evasive maneuvers, and when I thought the car was gone, I headed home.

I walked in, and before I could do anything, I felt the barrel of a gun on my back. And a voice said, "I knew you were a good inspector, but I never gave you credit for being such a great one. Now move and sit down."

I recognized the voice immediately. It was the chief. Her voice had a unique tone to it; once you hear it, you could never forget it.

"Chief, what is going on?" I asked at the same time that I called Fran, hoping she would pick up and figure out what was going on.

"I knew you would figure out about the horses the moment you walked into my office. And I had to stop you before you went any further," she said.

"How are you going to explain me getting killed in my house?" I asked.

"Very simple: the person who is after you and your sister finished the job. I will leave some subtle clues into the motive, and also, the woman who talked to you earlier this week, she is dead. I can't leave any loose ends. When they find you dead, there will be enough evidence to lead the investigation to her. They will find her dead. She would have committed suicide. There will be a note saying that she is sorry for killing you, her friend. The investigation of all this will go cold and no one will know that I was behind it all," she said.

"How are you going to kill me? Can you please explain all this?" I asked.

"It all has to do with my son. You saw his photo. When he came back from the war, he came back changed. His father and I tried to help him, but he got deep in with a gang. In reality, they were members of one of the most powerful drug cartels in Mexico. Once he got in with them, there was no way out. It was through him that I learned about them using horse racing as a form of money laundering. But I just could not help him get out. The more I tried, the deeper he got. Then one day he told me that if I did not help him with the horse smuggling ring and money laundering, they would kill his dad. I did not believe him. Two days later, my husband was in a car accident. He was dead on the spot. My son came back and confronted me. He said that if I did not help them, they would kill him. This time I believed them. Unfortunately, the more I helped, the deeper I got. Then one day, my son was found dead of an overdose. But by that time, I was in too deep to get out," she said.

"Why did you target my sister and me? We didn't know anything about the horse smuggling and money laundering. Why target us?" I asked.

By this time, I was hoping that Fran had gotten my call and was able to tape the conversation.

"I knew that sooner or later, you two would find each other and would, just as I thought, start working this case. That was something I could not afford. She had to go, but my man did not get the job done. Then I had to have Vargas killed. He was a link to my assassin. And with Vargas gone, so was Turner. Turner knew too much. Both Vargas and Turner had served with my son. They knew what was going on. They were both a liability, and I had them killed. Then things got messy. You and your sister started to put things together. You two became a much larger liability. So, you had to go. I ordered him to kill you, but once again, he failed. You ladies are ridiculously hard to kill. So…"

"I know, he had to go. I have another question—"

She interrupted. "NO MORE QUESTIONS," she screamed out.

"No, you owe me an answer, and I want answers," I said in a loud voice. "How did you know about Fran and me?" I asked.

"Have you ever heard of DNA?" she said, mocking me. "Turner said that his new boss looked very much like my new lieutenant. He had seen you at an activity in my office. You probably did not pay too much attention to him. At that time, you were still married to Tom. So, I confirmed his observation; we got hair from your brushes and got your DNA," she explained.

"But how did you get into my house? I have a very secure lock," I said.

"Not as secure as you thought," she said, then looking at me she very coldly said, "It is time to say good night."

"One more question before you kill me: why did you kill Dorothy, and just one more question, Is there anyone else in the department helping you?" I asked. I knew that I was trying to stretch the situation in the hopes that Fran had gotten the call and that the cavalry was on its way.

"Stop, I will answer this question and no more. No one is coming to help you; this is the end of the of the streetcar," she said, I needed someone to take the fall for your murder, and she was the perfect one. She had just spoken to you, and she was worried about the stable where she worked at. I know what your question is, How did I know about your conversation with her? Technology, your phone is tapped, and it goes straight to my office. And no, there is no one else in the department that knows about this. Remember what the saying is, 'The best way to keep a secret between three is when two are dead.' The more people who knew in the department, the more risk there was," she said.

Maybe she was right; the cavalry might not be coming, but I was still holding out hope until she pulled that trigger. But just as she was about to kill me, my door slammed open and there was Fran, gun in hand, followed by Peterson and several other officers.

"Put it down," she said in a very demanding voice, "If you shoot her, I will shoot you," she said.

"Chief, please put the gun down," Peterson said.

And in a split second, the chief turned the gun on herself and pulled the trigger. And with that action, she put an end to this nightmare.

I knew why she had killed herself. She was not going to go to jail, one way or another. She was going to end up dead. Better to do it by her own hand.

CHAPTER 11
A SOLUTION (?)

Several weeks had gone by after the incident in my house. The Internal Affairs investigation was exceedingly long, but it was important to know if there were any more corrupt cops in the department.

During the investigation, it gave me time to get to know my sister even more, to connect with my mother and that brother that had been a face on Skype. I got to meet my other sister-in-law and their kid. It also gave me time to reconnect with Tom. We decided to give us a second chance. It also gave me a chance to really reconnect with my friend Claire.

Peterson was promoted to sergeant. I was promoted to chief of detectives. Things seemed to be going very well. But in the back of my mind, there was a lingering thought about the fact that there was still someone out there pulling the strings to this operation. It looked like it was over, but I knew deep down it wasn't over.

Then one day, an envelope was left on my desk. The message inside was simple and yet overly complicated. It read:

"YOU CAN CUT THE HEAD OFF A HYDRA, BUT A NEW ONE WILL GROW IN ITS PLACE. BEWARE!"